THE FOUR Rs of CYBERSECURITY

SCOTT GOLDMAN

The Four Rs
of
Cybersecurity

A step-by-step guide for CEOs,
Board Directors, and other non-geeks

What to ask, what to know, and
what to ignore

by

Scott Goldman

SCOTT GOLDMAN, PUBLISHER

ISBN 979-8-35092-743-6

My eternal thanks for this book design to my dear friend and
collaborator, Ed Legum of Nashville. I quite literally
could not have done this without him.

CONTENTS

DEDICATION

This book is dedicated to my friend, mentor, and cheerleader, Harvey. His encouragement and ability to impart profound wisdom with charm, wit, and patience have helped drive and guide me toward greater success and happiness than I could have achieved on my own. I am eternally grateful for all he has done for me.

ACKNOWLEDGMENTS

Allow me to take this opportunity to thank a bunch of people who have helped along the way, not just with this, my third book, but also with the day-to-day things that give me the time and freedom to pursue endeavors like this.

First and foremost, my amazing, supportive, encouraging, and loving wife, Debra. I could go on for more pages than there are in this book about what she means to me – marrying her was the single smartest decision I've ever made.

To my family of smart, witty, happy, fun, and enjoyable people who show me love and accept mine: Nicole, Lucky, Shaun, Laz and Ruby, Raja and Nicholas. And to my unofficial family members Jesse and Jared – I love you all.

A special thanks to my wonderful cousins Barbara, Mindy and Sheila, who, through their endless love and support, have become like siblings to me. To the rest of my awesome family – you all make my life better in your own individual way and I am so grateful for it..

I owe special gratitude to my incredible group of close friends, whose patience and support have been invaluable. Whether discussing things over dinner, laughing over beers, or chatting while biking side by side for mile upon happy mile, life would be far less complete without you. Andy, Jack, and Leelo – my longest-time buddies who are amazing and the best pals a guy like me could ever hope to find. And to my pals Alan, Jeff and Todd - you've proven time and again that although we've ridden thousands of miles side-by-side, it's not about the bike. Thank you for everything. And of course, to friends Avi, Dennis, Emilio, Izzy, Jamie, Joerg, Howard (FIL and N.), Matt, Mitch, Neal, Paul (B. and G.), Robbie (ok - Rob), Sandy, Stacey (a special hat-tip for suggestions and guidance for this book's cover), Stan, Teena, Wendy and Yossi – you are all proof that friends are the family you get to choose. You are the best.

To my business associates, who contribute to the pleasure of work every day and are a joy to work with; Mark,

Dee, Charles, Kenny, Therese, and Coleen – the TextPower team – thank you for making every day fun, productive and thought-provoking.

To my fellow Mueller Industries, Inc. board directors Bill, Chuck, Gary, John, Lisa, Terry and retired members John F. and Paul. And to the brilliant and dedicated executive team of Greg, Jeff, Chris and Stefan, our sagacious counsel Serge, the ever-helpful Mandy and so many others at Mueller Industries, Inc., you all inspire me to continually strive for excellence in my life. Thank you for that.

Finally, to all the service and delivery people who deliver packages and food, maintain my bikes, occasionally walk my pal Gadget and keep the house tidy – thank you. Without you, I would have to do all of it myself, and this book would never have been completed!

FOREWORD

AS THE CEO of a global enterprise of businesses, I am often asked what keeps me up at night. While the challenges our company confronts are always changing, one primary and persistent concern — particularly in today's environment — is how best to balance the opportunities and risks associated with technology. Without a doubt, technology permeates everything we do. It enables us to connect, communicate and to operate with enhanced speed, efficiency, precision and effectiveness. Like all business leaders, one of my core responsibilities is to unlock the full potential of innovation to improve the bottom line. That said, business leaders must also understand and guard against the rapidly evolving security threats presented by technology, including the threat actors who continually seek creative ways to deceive our employees, penetrate our systems and steal our critical information.

With news headlines of major cybersecurity breaches rolling in on a near weekly basis, I am amazed at just how vulnerable we have all become. Today, some of the most mundane tasks, like sending an email or paying a bill, have become fraught with risk. The stories are enough to make any business leader feel, to a degree, powerless, or that a breach is an inevitability. But neither is the case. Quite the contrary, there are many proactive measures we can take to identify gaps in our defenses, secure our systems, educate our workforces and mitigate our cybersecurity risk. And that is why I believe this book to be such an important must read.

The Four Rs of Cybersecurity distills complex concepts into practical insights. It offers guidance on strengthening cybersecurity practices and reducing risks, and does so with language and examples that everyone can understand, irrespective of their level of technological savvy. Particularly, it equips CEOs, corporate boards of directors, executives and operational business leaders with the knowledge and tools needed to meet their fiduciary obligations. Armed with this information, business leaders are better prepared, educated and empowered to understand how to protect their organizations' assets in a perilous digital landscape.

Gregory L. Christopher
Chairman & CEO, Mueller Industries, Inc.

INTRODUCTION

BACK IN 1986 two brothers had a clever idea to stop customers from stealing their software. They wrote a bit of code to prevent people from illegally copying it and hid it on the floppy disks they used to distribute their software. Unfortunately they couldn't anticipate the unintended negative consequences of that effort. That bit of code ended up spreading everywhere, eventually infecting computers that didn't even have their software, weren't connected to any network and had zero clue about what was happening. Computers around the world started spending their time and processing power replicating and spreading the copy-prevention software instead of performing their intended tasks. As a result they all slowed to a crawl – and the cybersecurity industry was born.

This one small action shocked people into realizing how quickly computer viruses spread. It changed, virtually overnight, how people and enterprises saw the need for antivirus cybersecurity awareness, antivirus software, preventing hackers and backing up data.

Today, 30+ years later, too many of us are still insufficiently aware of the risks, consequences and need to protect against cyberattacks. Cybersecurity discussions can be intimidating and complex – but there's a desperate need to make the topic simple and understandable. This applies to people at the top of the food chain in enterprises and small businesses alike. Owners, CEOs, board directors and others with responsibilities to employees, customers and shareholders must be cyberaware.

That's what this book is about.

Let me start by saying that if you can already distinguish a virus from a trojan or a packet sniffer from a firewall, this book is not for you. You'd find more value in taking cooking lessons or learning how to crochet. On the other hand, if you're not directly involved in cybersecurity or just an individual seeking insight into why the bad guys seem to be constantly outsmarting the good guys, you've come to the right place.

The fundamental issue surrounding cybersecurity is pretty simple, actually – it has historically been an afterthought for most company leaders and even the general population. Generally speaking, we all had our roles within the organizations we worked for and seldom ventured beyond them. CEOs led the way, CFOs managed finances, and HR teams dealt with personnel matters. But in today's business landscape, cybersecurity transcends boundaries. It has become a fundamental aspect of every business that every position within an organization must grapple with and take responsibility for. At its core, cybersecurity represents a mindset and attitude that should permeate the culture and fabric of every organization.

Unfortunately, this transformation hasn't fully materialized yet. It's hardly surprising when we consider the laser focus and specialization inherent in our respective roles. Consider board directors, for instance. While some perceive directors as sitting atop the corporate hierarchy, they actually occupy a unique position within the companies they serve. While they are tasked with providing oversight, guidance, and counsel to the CEOs who report to them, they (typically) aren't employees and aren't expected to possess extensive expertise in the company's core operations. A board director at General Motors wouldn't be expected to comprehend the intricate details of building a fuel injection system, just as a director at Nvidia wouldn't be expected to know where to begin designing a microchip.

However, it has recently become the directors' job to question the cybersecurity capabilities and require that executives give it sufficient attention. How can one do that without a fundamental understanding of what they're asking of the company's executives?

Moreover, as our working world continues to subdivide roles into increasingly specialized domains, general knowledge about overall business operations diminishes. Individuals may specialize in finance, acquisitions, manufacturing processes or real estate, but few possess expertise in the one area that now affects every company, director, and C-level executive in today's business world – cybersecurity. This reality must change, and this book aims to facilitate that change. We all need to comprehend the essential elements of cybersecurity, know how to acquire the information we need, and understand the right questions to ask. It's high time we step out of the realm of unfamiliarity and take charge.

Now, let's delve into why this subject holds immense significance. Just take a glance at current news headlines on almost any day and you'll witness the profound impact that hacking, security breaches, stolen credentials, and defaced websites can have on a company's financial standing and reputation. The costs are substantial by any measure and devastating in more than a few. Let's work together to stop that – NOW.

THE "FOUR Rs" OF CYBERSECURITY

WHILE CYBERSECURITY is a complex, deeply involved, and evolving topic, it can be demystified. In fact, when you distill all the available information, everything you need to understand about protecting your company (or yourself) from attacks and recovering from them when they occur falls under four clear categories. Let's dive into the "Four Rs" of cybersecurity:

- *Resist*
- *Restrict*
- *Recover*
- *Report*

Understand the fundamentals behind these four Rs, and you'll be miles ahead of your fellow C-Suite executives and directors. Importantly, the companies you work for will benefit from your knowledge in a way that helps keep them ahead of the competition. You don't have to know a lot – just the basics – so I've tried to keep things at a high-level overview. Occasionally you'll see "DEEP DIVE" on a topic and you can read more about it if you want to, or skip it if you think you've got the general idea.

In essence, knowing more about cybersecurity is another way of managing risk, which can be expressed as a Risk Formula, as seen in the graphic above.

As you read this book, this formula will make more and more sense. And how do the Four Rs relate to this critical formula?

- Resistance reduces the threat of breaches.
- Restrictions lower your vulnerability.
- Recovery reduces the impact of a breach.
- Reporting is something you'll be glad to do if you've followed the first three Rs.

RESIST

PROTECTION, IN ITS MOST FUNDAMENTAL FORM, is about resistance. If you're securing a house, you'll want strong locks. A boxer resists getting knocked out by blocking punches. Similarly, an enterprise trying to prevent cyberattacks must first resist the attack. But how can an enterprise resist the attacks that come at it daily or, in some cases, by the minute and still keep data intact and flowing when needed? (Want to be astonished? You can see a live cyberthreat map here: https://threatmap.checkpoint.com)

In cybersecurity, resistance refers to the ability of a system or network to withstand and defend against various threats and attacks. It involves the measures put in place to prevent unauthorized access, data breaches, and other malicious activities.

Think of resistance as the security measures that protect your digital assets, similar to how locks and alarms protect physical property. These measures can include things like strong passwords, encryption, firewalls, and antivirus software – all of which are explained in understandable language further into this book. By implementing robust resistance strategies, organizations and individuals can reduce the risk of cyberattacks and minimize potential damage. It's an essential aspect of maintaining a secure and trusted digital environment.

However, the first thing to understand is that not every attack will be resisted or repelled. Let's compare your enterprise's computer system and network to a household. In terms of security measures, you'll want solid deadbolt locks and strong doors and windows at a minimum. But what about lighting? Motion detecting security lights? An alarm system? A dog? What about the last line of defense? Do you want to keep a firearm in the house for personal protection?

Whatever you decide, the ultimate goal is for every additional layer of security to make it increasingly difficult for someone to break into your house or do you harm. In the end, your best bet is to make your home so difficult or risky to break into that criminals decide to pass on your place and go next door.

It's the same with cyber protection. Your strategy should be to make it as difficult as possible for someone to gain access, find valuable data, encrypt files, or do damage such that all but the most persistent intruders will try somewhere else.

HOW THE HACKERS WILL HACK

1 BUSINESS EMAIL COMPROMISE (BEC)

This is the single most common method of hackers breaching your network. It refers to a type of cyberattack where attackers manipulate or compromise legitimate email accounts within an organization to carry out fraudulent activities. It typically involves impersonating a trusted individual, such as a company executive or a business partner, to deceive employees, customers, or vendors into taking unauthorized actions or revealing sensitive information.

Here's how a typical BEC attack works:

1.1 *Reconnaissance*. Attackers gather information about the targeted organization, its key personnel, and business relationships. They may conduct research through publicly available sources, social media, or previous data breaches.

1.2 *Social Engineering*. Attackers employ social engineering techniques to trick individuals into taking specific actions. This can include sending urgent requests for fund transfers, invoice payments, or sensitive data, often accompanied by a sense of urgency, authority, or confidentiality.

1.3 *Compromised Accounts*. In some cases, attackers gain unauthorized access to legitimate email accounts through techniques like phishing, credential theft, or malware. By controlling these compromised accounts, they can send fraudulent emails and further deceive recipients.

The damage caused by BEC attacks can be significant and

can include financial loss, the breach of sensitive data, such as financial information, customer data, or intellectual property. Reputational damage can be significant, too. Falling victim to a BEC attack can damage the organization's reputation and erode trust with customers, partners, and stakeholders. It may be perceived as a sign of weak security practices or insufficient controls, impacting relationships and business opportunities. Finally, there are potential legal and compliance issues. If personal or sensitive data is compromised in a BEC attack, the targeted organization may face legal consequences or violations of data protection and privacy regulations. Failure to protect customer or employee information can result in lawsuits, fines, or other legal liabilities.

BEC can be avoided – or at least minimized – by following the protective procedures found later in this book.

2 TYPES OF EMAIL PHISHING ATTACKS

You can be "phished" by a blast message that goes out to everyone in your team, department, or company. This method is a way of "spamming" everyone on a list in the hope that the law of large numbers will take over and at least one of the recipients will click a link, download a nefarious file, or take some other action that allows the hackers to access your network. There are subcategories of email phishing, too:

2.1 *Phishing*. You might recognize this among the "spam" that everyone typically filters into their spam folder. Cybercriminals send emails or messages that appear to be from trustworthy sources, like banks or reputable companies, to trick people into revealing sensitive information such as passwords, credit card details, or social security numbers. What happens here is that the sender is trying to get you to click on a link that leads to a form that looks like a legitimate website (bank sites, shopping platforms, and social media login pages are the most often imitated). Once you've landed on that page, any information you enter, such as your ID, password, or social security number, is stolen by the hackers and

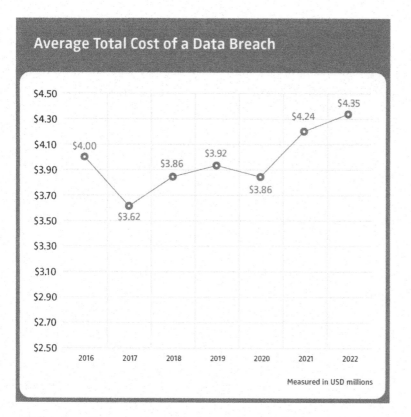

Average Total Cost of a Data Breach

Measured in USD millions

sold online. However, remember that not all spam emails are phishing attempts. A lot of them are from legitimate companies that simply blast millions of emails because it's cheap and easy and even a tiny response rate can make it profitable.

2.2 *Spearphishing.* In this specialized form of phishing, an email is sent specifically to one or more people that the hacker thinks will be responsive to their message. The benefit of using spearphishing is, by its definition, limited and, as a result, is less likely to raise alarms.

2.3 *Spoofing.* In this type of phishing, an email is sent that appears to come from someone at a high level in the company. Spoofing an email address is a trivial matter, so hackers use this method all the time. For example, if someone in the accounting department were to receive a message from a random employee directing them to make a payment, it might not be very effective. However, if the message was "spoofed" so that it appeared to come from the CFO, the accountant might think it was a legitimate request and send that payment without verifying it in an attempt to leave a good impression about how speedy they are.

3 MORE SOPHISTICATED CYBER ATTACKS

So I should watch out for some bad links and emails, but what's the big deal? Doesn't everyone do that already? Actually, no. There are so many different ways for hackers to attack and break into your system (also known as attack "vectors"). Let's help you understand them a bit more here.

What are the different methods a hacker might capitalize on to penetrate your company's network? They fall into a few categories:

3.1 *Malware.* Malware is malicious software that can harm your computer or network. It includes viruses, worms, trojans, other assorted bad stuff, and possibly the worst of all – ransomware. Ransomware can be hidden in files or websites and, when activated, can steal information, damage systems, or lock your files until a ransom is paid.

3.2 *Denial-of-Service* **(DoS)** *Attacks.* Imagine a shop being flooded with more customers than it can handle, causing chaos and preventing others from entering. In a DoS attack, hackers overwhelm a website or network with excessive traffic, making it inaccessible to legitimate users.

❖ DEEP DIVE

▸ *A Distributed Denial of Service* (DDoS) *Attack.* This is a malicious attempt to disrupt the normal functioning of a network, service, or website by overwhelming it with a flood of illegitimate traffic. In a DDoS attack, multiple compromised computers or devices, known as botnets, are coordinated to send a massive volume of requests or data to the targeted system simultaneously. This is done in an effort to overwhelm the system and render it unable to handle legitimate user requests. DDoS attacks can be highly disruptive and have various objectives, including:

▸ *Denying Service.* The primary goal of a DDoS attack is to render a targeted system or service unavailable to legitimate users. By overwhelming the system's resources, such as bandwidth, processing power, or memory, the attacker aims to interrupt or disrupt normal operations.

▸ *Distraction.* DDoS attacks may also be used as a diversionary tactic to divert attention and resources from other malicious activities, such as data breaches or unauthorized access attempts.

▸ *Extortion or Revenge.* In some cases, attackers launch DDoS attacks to extort money from targeted organizations, threatening to continue the attack unless a ransom is paid. DDoS attacks can also be motivated by revenge or as a means of causing reputational damage to a targeted entity.

▸ *Protecting Against DDoS Attacks.* Organizations can employ several strategies to avoid or mitigate the impact of a DDoS attack:

• DDoS Mitigation Services. Engaging with a reputable DDoS mitigation service can provide specialized expertise and infrastructure to detect and mitigate DDoS attacks. These services utilize various techniques, such as traffic filtering, rate limiting, and load balancing, to divert and absorb malicious traffic while allowing legitimate traffic to reach the target.

• Network & Infrastructure Protection. Implementing network and infrastructure security measures can help defend against DDoS attacks. This includes utilizing firewalls, intrusion prevention systems (IPSs), and load balancers to filter and manage incoming traffic by identifying and blocking suspicious or anomalous traffic patterns.

• Traffic Monitoring and Anomaly Detection. Employing robust monitoring systems that can analyze network traffic in real time can help identify and detect potential DDoS attacks. Anomaly detection algorithms can flag abnormal traffic patterns, allowing for swift response and mitigation.

‣ Scalable Infrastructure. Building a scalable and resilient network infrastructure with sufficient bandwidth and processing power can help absorb and handle increased traffic during a DDoS attack. Load balancing and distributed server architectures distribute the load and minimize the impact on individual systems.

‣ Incident Response Planning. Developing a comprehensive incident response plan that includes specific protocols and procedures for handling DDoS attacks is crucial. This plan should define roles, responsibilities, and escalation paths, all of which will enable organizations to respond effectively during an attack.

‣ Redundancy & Failover Mechanisms. Implementing redundancy and failover mechanisms ensures that critical systems or services have backup resources available. This allows for quick recovery and minimizes the impact of an ongoing DDoS attack.

It's important to note that DDoS attacks can be highly complex and can vary in scale and sophistication. Combining multiple preventive measures, continuous monitoring, and a swift response is key to minimizing the impact and disruption they cause.

4 MAN-IN-THE-MIDDLE (MITM) ATTACKS

Think of MiTM attacks as eavesdropping during a private conversation. Attackers position themselves between two parties communicating on a network, intercepting and potentially altering the communication without either party realizing it. This allows them to steal information or even manipulate the conversation.

5 SQL INJECTION

Imagine a burglar exploiting a weak lock to gain unauthorized access to a building. In SQL injection attacks, hackers take advantage of poorly coded websites by injecting malicious SQL code into input fields. This code manipulates the website's database, potentially revealing sensitive information.

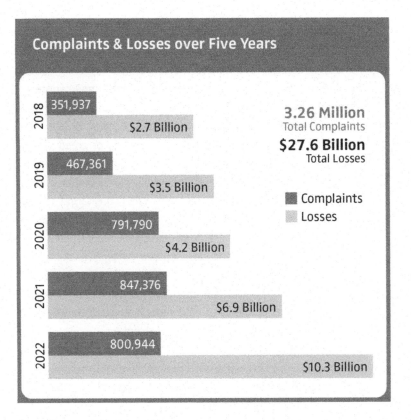

Complaints & Losses over Five Years

2018 351,937 — $2.7 Billion
2019 467,361 — $3.5 Billion
2020 791,790 — $4.2 Billion
2021 847,376 — $6.9 Billion
2022 800,944 — $10.3 Billion

3.26 Million Total Complaints
$27.6 Billion Total Losses

■ Complaints
■ Losses

6 SOCIAL ENGINEERING

Social engineering attacks involve manipulating people rather than exploiting technical vulnerabilities. These attacks prey on human trust and emotions to trick individuals into revealing sensitive information or performing actions that may compromise security.

> ❖ DEEP DIVE
> Social Engineering is a technique used by individuals or groups to manipulate and deceive people into performing certain actions or divulging sensitive information. It exploits the inherent trust and natural human inclination to help others, making it a powerful tool for malicious purposes. There are several forms of social engineering, each with its own characteristics and dangers.

Here are some of the most common forms:

6.1 *Pretexting*. Pretexting involves creating a fabricated scenario or pretext to manipulate the target into revealing sensitive information. For example, an attacker might impersonate a co-worker, government official, or customer support representative to extract information like passwords or account details.

6.2 *Baiting*. Baiting relies on human curiosity or greed by offering the target something desirable or enticing. This can be in the form of infected USB drives left in public places or fake download links promising exclusive content. When the target takes the bait, malware is installed, or other malicious actions are initiated.

6.3 *Tailgating*. Tailgating, also known as piggybacking, involves an attacker gaining unauthorized access to a restricted area by following closely behind an authorized person. This exploits the natural tendency to hold doors open for others or not question someone's presence in a secure location.

6.4 *Impersonation*. Impersonation involves pretending to be someone else to gain trust and access sensitive information. This can include impersonating a colleague, a company executive, or even a law enforcement officer.

6.5 *Quid Pro Quo*. In this technique, the attacker promises something of value to the target in exchange for information or access. For example, an attacker might offer a free gift or a service upgrade in return for login credentials or other sensitive data.

6.6 *Reverse Social Engineering*. Reverse social engineering flips the script by convincing the target that they need help or assistance from the attacker. The attacker gains the target's trust by offering technical support, claiming to fix a problem, or providing expertise. In reality, the attacker is trying to extract sensitive information or gain unauthorized access.

6.7 *Stopping Social Engineering*. Attacks can be challenging for several reasons.

▸ *Human Vulnerability*. Social engineering exploits human

psychology and emotions, making it difficult to defend against. People are generally trusting, helpful, and susceptible to manipulation, especially when caught off guard or under pressure.

▸ *Constant Evolution*. Social engineering techniques are continually evolving. Attackers adapt their strategies, leveraging current events, technologies, and cultural trends. This makes it challenging for security measures to keep up.

▸ *Complexity of Detection*. Social engineering attacks often involve deception and manipulation, making them difficult to detect using automated security systems alone. Attackers can bypass technical defenses by exploiting human vulnerabilities.

6.8 *The Dangers* presented by social engineering are significant.

▸ *Unauthorized Access*. Social engineering attacks can result in unauthorized access to systems, networks, or physical locations. Attackers can gain control over sensitive information, manipulate data, or cause damage to infrastructure.

▸ *Data Breaches*. Social engineering attacks can lead to data breaches by tricking individuals into divulging sensitive information, resulting in identity theft, financial losses, or reputational damage for individuals or organizations.

▸ *Malware and Ransomware*. Social engineering attacks often involve the distribution of malware or ransomware. Once the victim falls for the deception and interacts with the malicious payload, their system may be compromised, leading to further data theft, financial extortion, or operational disruption.

▸ *Financial Fraud*. Attackers can exploit social engineering techniques to commit financial fraud. This includes stealing credit card information, conducting unauthorized transactions, or tricking individuals into wiring money to fraudulent accounts.

6.9 *To Mitigate the Dangers* of social engineering, it is crucial to raise awareness and provide education on recognizing and responding to social engineering attacks. This includes promoting skepticism, encouraging individuals to verify requests independently, and implementing strong security practices such as multi-factor authentication and regular security awareness training. Organizations should also focus on creating a security culture that emphasizes vigilance, caution, and the importance of reporting suspicious activities.

7 ZERO-DAY EXPLOITS

A zero-day exploit is an attack that happens as soon as a new vulnerability is discovered and before anyone has had the time to develop a patch to fix it. Cybercriminals leverage these vulnerabilities to target systems that are not yet protected, making it challenging for organizations to defend against such attacks.

8 CREDENTIAL-STUFFING

Imagine you have a bunch of keys, and you know that many people use the same key for multiple doors, like their home, office, or car. In a credential-stuffing attack, hackers take advantage of this behavior. They collect a large number of stolen username and password combinations from one source (like a data breach) and try using those combinations on multiple websites and online services. Since people often reuse their credentials, the hackers hope to find a match. Just like trying different keys in multiple locks, the hackers use automated tools to rapidly input the stolen username and password combinations into different websites, hoping to gain unauthorized access to user accounts.

9 KEYLOGGERS

A keylogger, also known as a keystroke logger, is a type of malicious software or hardware device designed to record and monitor keystrokes typed on a computer or mobile device. It captures and logs every key pressed, including passwords, credit card information, chat conversations, and other sensitive data.

❖ DEEP DIVE

Keyloggers can infiltrate a computer through various means:

9.1 *Malware Infection*. Keyloggers often come bundled with malware such as trojans or spyware. They can be downloaded unknowingly when users visit compromised websites, open malicious email attachments, or install infected software from unreliable sources.

9.2 *Physical Access*. Hardware-based keyloggers can be physically installed on a computer by an attacker who gains physical access to the device. These keyloggers are often inserted between the keyboard and the computer or installed inside the computer case.

9.3 *The Risks* associated with keyloggers are significant.

▸ *Privacy Breach*. Keyloggers can capture personal and sensitive information, leading to privacy breaches and identity theft. Attackers can gain access to usernames, passwords, financial details, and other confidential information.

▸ *Financial Loss*. If keyloggers capture banking or credit card information, attackers can use the stolen data for fraudulent transactions or unauthorized access to financial accounts, resulting in financial loss for the victim.

▸ *Unauthorized Access*. Keyloggers can capture login credentials for various accounts, giving attackers the ability to gain unauthorized access to email accounts, social media profiles, online services, or company networks.

10 REMOVING A KEYLOGGER

Removing a keylogger from a computer requires immediate action:

10.1 *Use Anti-Malware Software*. Run a thorough scan using reputable antivirus or anti-malware software to detect and remove the keylogger. Ensure your security software is up to date to identify the latest threats.

10.2 *Update Operating System and Applications*. Keep your

operating system and applications updated with the latest security patches. This helps mitigate vulnerabilities that keyloggers may exploit.

10.3 *Change Passwords.* As a precaution, change passwords for all critical accounts, including email, online banking, and social media platforms. Choose strong and unique passwords to enhance security.

10.4 **Enable Two-Factor Authentication** (*2FA*). Enable 2FA on your accounts whenever possible. This adds an extra layer of security, making it difficult for attackers to gain unauthorized access even if they have captured your login credentials.

10.5 *Be Cautious & Educated.* Be vigilant while downloading software, opening attachments, or clicking on links. Avoid suspicious websites, emails from unknown sources, and unverified software sources.

If you suspect a keylogger, it is recommended to seek assistance from a cybersecurity professional who can perform a thorough investigation and provide guidance on removing the keylogger effectively.

11 API VULNERABILITIES

Let's start with a basic explanation of an API (Application Programming Interface) before discussing API vulnerabilities.

An API, or Application Programming Interface, is like a set of rules and protocols that allow different software applications to interact and communicate with each other. It acts as a bridge or intermediary, enabling applications to share data, functionality, and services with each other.

To put it in simpler terms, imagine you want to order food from a restaurant. The restaurant's menu is like the API, providing you with a list of available dishes and their descriptions. You, as the customer, can make specific requests by ordering from the menu, and the restaurant's kitchen (the application) will receive those requests and prepare the food accordingly. The API facilitates this communication between you (the customer) and the restaurant (the application).

In the digital world, APIs work similarly. They define the methods and rules that applications use to communicate and exchange data. For example, social media platforms like Facebook and Twitter provide APIs that allow other applications or developers to integrate features like logging in with Facebook or sharing content on Twitter. This enables developers to leverage the functionality and data of these platforms in their own applications.

Or imagine you have a house with a front door that you use to interact with the outside world. Now, think of an API (Application Programming Interface) as a special door or entrance that allows different software applications to communicate and share information with each other.

An API vulnerability occurs when there's a weakness or flaw in the way this special door (API) is designed or implemented, allowing someone with malicious intent to exploit this weakness and gain unauthorized access to sensitive data or perform harmful actions within a system or application.

What makes API vulnerabilities particularly risky is that they often go unnoticed or overlooked by companies. Companies often focus on securing their main doors, such as their websites or user interfaces, while forgetting about the APIs they use to connect with other applications or services. This lack of attention leaves API vulnerabilities as a potential attack vector that attackers can exploit.

When attackers identify an API vulnerability, they can manipulate or bypass security controls, access restricted information, modify data, or even perform unauthorized actions within an application or system. This can have severe consequences, such as:

11.1 *Data Breaches*. API vulnerabilities can lead to unauthorized access to sensitive data, such as personal information, financial records, or confidential business data. Attackers can steal, manipulate, or expose this information, potentially causing financial loss, reputational damage, or legal consequences.

11.2 *System Compromise*. Exploiting an API vulnerability can allow attackers to take control of an application, system, or network. They can inject malicious code, install malware, or disrupt the normal functioning of an application or system, leading to service interruptions or loss of data.

11.3 *Unauthorized Actions*. Attackers can use API vulnerabilities to perform actions they shouldn't be able to, such as creating, modifying, or deleting data, initiating fraudulent transactions, or bypassing security controls. These unauthorized actions can lead to financial fraud, identity theft, or system or process manipulation.

To ensure robust security, it is important for companies to consider API vulnerabilities and implement proper security measures. This includes conducting regular security assessments, implementing secure coding practices, performing vulnerability testing, and ensuring that APIs are properly authenticated, authorized, and monitored. By addressing API vulnerabilities proactively, companies can prevent unauthorized access or data breaches and protect their systems, data, and reputation.

12 SOFTWARE

This is probably the biggest category among all types of resistance, including everything from spam filters (available in both hardware and software formats, sometimes as a combination from the same vendor) to virus and malware scanners to automated patching for your chosen software programs. You really don't have to know a lot about the software that's available to do this, just that there is a wide variety of it and your job is to ask whether or not it's been installed and kept updated. But if you really want to know more about it, please read the "Deep Dive" section that follows.

❖ DEEP DIVE

Different types of software play crucial roles in helping an enterprise resist cyberattacks by providing specific security functionalities. When combined with hardware and proper security practices, these software solutions contribute to a comprehensive cybersecurity strategy. They help enterprises protect against a wide range of cyber threats, including malware infections, network intrusions, data breaches, and unauthorized access. Implementing a combination of software-based security measures enhances an organization's ability to detect, prevent, and respond to cyberattacks, safeguarding critical assets and maintaining a strong security posture. Here are some examples.

12.1 *Antivirus & Anti-Malware Software*. Antivirus and anti-malware software are designed to detect, prevent, and remove malicious software, such as viruses, worms, trojans, and ransomware. These software solutions scan files, programs, and system memory for known signatures or suspicious behavior, blocking or quarantining potential threats. Regular updates keep the software's database of malware definitions up to date to effectively combat emerging threats.

12.2 *Security Information & Event Management* (*SIEM*) *Systems*. SIEM software collects, analyzes, and correlates security event logs from various sources within an enterprise's network. These sources include firewalls, servers, routers, and other security devices. SIEM systems provide real-time monitoring, threat detection, log correlation, and reporting capabilities. By aggregating and correlating security events, they help identify potential threats, facilitate timely incident response, and enable compliance monitoring.

12.3 *Endpoint Protection Software*. Endpoint protection software, often referred to as endpoint security solutions, safeguards endpoints such as desktops, laptops, and mobile devices from a wide range of threats. These solutions include features such as antivirus, anti-malware, host-based intrusion detection, firewall, data encryption, and device control, ultimately helping prevent unauthorized access, detect and block malicious activities, and protect sensitive data on individual devices.

12.4 *Patch Management Software.* Patch management software helps ensure that operating systems, applications, and software components are up to date with the latest security patches and updates. It automates the process of identifying, downloading, and deploying patches across an enterprise's systems, reducing vulnerabilities and minimizing the risk of exploitation by known vulnerabilities.

12.5 *Encryption Software.* Encryption software is used to protect sensitive data by converting it into unreadable ciphertext that can only be decrypted with the correct encryption keys. It helps ensure the confidentiality and integrity of data, especially during transit or when stored on devices or in the cloud. Encryption software provides an additional layer of protection in case of unauthorized access or data breaches.

13 HARDWARE

This is where you'll find firewalls, spam filters, and security keys as physical components to be added to your network. Companies sell these components for enterprises of all sizes, and there are dozens of reputable vendors. You, as a director or CLE (C-Level Executive), don't need to know all about them; you just need to know that they exist and that you'll need them.

❖ DEEP DIVE

Hardware devices can enhance an enterprise's resilience against cyber threats by providing network segmentation, traffic filtering, threat detection, secure authentication, and centralized monitoring capabilities. By deploying a combination of hardware and software security measures, organizations can better protect their networks, systems, and data from a wide range of cyberattacks. The following types of hardware devices contribute to a layered defense strategy.

13.1 *Firewalls*. Firewalls are network security devices that act as a barrier between internal and external networks, such as the internet. They monitor incoming and outgoing network traffic, applying predefined security rules to filter and block potentially malicious traffic. Firewalls help prevent unauthorized access, protect against network-based attacks, and ensure secure communication.

13.2 *Intrusion Detection & Prevention Systems (IDPS)*. IDPS devices and their associated software are designed to detect and respond to potential cyber threats by monitoring network traffic and analyzing it for signs of malicious activities or known attack patterns. IDPS devices can identify and alert administrators about suspicious behavior, such as network intrusions or attempted exploits. Some IDPS systems can also automatically block or mitigate threats in real time.

13.3 *Security Information & Event Management (SIEM) Systems*. SIEM systems are hardware/software solutions that centralize and analyze security event logs from various sources within an enterprise's network. These sources include firewalls, servers, routers, and other security devices. SIEM systems provide real-time monitoring, threat detection, log correlation, and reporting capabilities. By aggregating and correlating security events, they help identify potential threats and facilitate timely incident response.

13.4 *Secure Hardware Tokens & Smart Cards*. Hardware tokens and smart cards are physical devices that store and generate unique cryptographic keys and credentials. They provide an additional layer of authentication and help protect against unauthorized access to sensitive systems and data. These tokens often require physical possession or user interaction to generate one-time passwords or cryptographic signatures, making it difficult for attackers to gain unauthorized access even if they possess stolen credentials.

13.5 *Security Keys for Multi-Factor Authentication (MFA)*. Security keys, such as Universal 2nd Factor (U2F) devices, are hardware tokens used for strong multi-factor authentication. They provide an extra layer of security beyond passwords by requiring users to physically possess and connect the security key to authenticate their identity. Security keys offer protection against phishing attacks and account compromise by ensuring that only the legitimate user with the physical key can access protected systems or accounts.

14 CULTURE & EDUCATION

If cybersecurity isn't baked into the company's culture, no amount of investment into hardware or software will matter. Your people have to be educated to be cyber-aware in the same way that they learned to put their seat belts on when driving.

14.1 *The Human Element*. Employees are the first line of defense against cyber threats. Cybercriminals frequently exploit human vulnerabilities through techniques like social engineering or phishing attacks. By fostering a cybersecurity-conscious culture, organizations can empower employees to be more vigilant, skeptical, and cautious when interacting with potential threats. A strong company culture promotes a sense of responsibility and encourages employees to report suspicious activities promptly, thereby minimizing the risk of successful attacks.

14.2 *Awareness & Knowledge*. Cybersecurity training and

education programs equip employees with the knowledge and skills necessary to identify and respond to cyber threats. They provide insights into common attack vectors, current trends in cybercrime, and best practices for secure behavior. With regular training, employees become aware of potential risks, understand the importance of cybersecurity measures, and learn how to adopt secure practices in their day-to-day work. This awareness helps create a more informed and security-conscious workforce, reducing the likelihood of falling victim to attacks.

14.3 *Incident Response Readiness*. Training programs often include incident response exercises and simulations. These exercises help employees understand their roles and responsibilities during a cyber incident, enabling them to respond effectively and efficiently. By practicing response scenarios, employees become familiar with the steps to take, whom to contact, and how to mitigate the impact of an attack. This preparedness minimizes confusion, allows for rapid response, and helps contain and mitigate the effects of an incident.

14.4 *Compliance & Policy Adherence*. Company culture, training, and education play a crucial role in ensuring compliance with regulatory requirements and internal security policies. Compliance frameworks often mandate regular employee training on cybersecurity practices. By integrating compliance requirements into the company culture and training programs, organizations ensure that employees are aware of their obligations and follow the prescribed security protocols. This reduces the risk of non-compliance penalties and strengthens the overall security posture.

14.5 *Continuous Improvement*. Company culture, training, and education foster a culture of continuous improvement in cybersecurity practices. Cyber threats evolve rapidly, and new vulnerabilities emerge regularly. By instilling a mindset of continuous learning and improvement, organizations can adapt to emerging threats and implement up-to-date security measures. Training programs can be updated to address

new attack vectors, technological advancements, and indus-
try-specific risks, enabling employees to stay ahead of potential threats.

15 GOOD HABITS

The easiest and most effective form of protection is simple –
you must instill good habits in the daily operations of your
team. For example:

15.1 ***Check it out with a phone call.*** Don't believe that an
email has come from someone just because the return address
says it does. This is easy to fake (or "spoof" in hacker terms)
and is used all the time in "phishing" attacks. For example,
if someone in your accounting department receives an unexpected email seemingly from the CEO or CFO directing
them to make a payment to a vendor or individual, it might
not have come from them. In such cases, the fastest, simplest,
and easiest thing to do is just pick up the phone to confirm it.
One phone call could save the company thousands – or more.

15.2 ***Sneaky Links.*** Just because it looks like a safe link doesn't
mean that it is a safe link. Here's a best practice – don't click
links in emails. No matter what the link says on-screen, it may
not actually lead to that location. (If you're reading this on
your computer instead of on paper, click this one, for example: www.FaceBook.com. It looks pretty innocent to anyone
who sees it, but if you click on it, you'll see that it doesn't lead
to where you expect at all. In this case, I've directed it to another benign site, but it could have taken you anywhere, such
as to a site that looks like your bank's home page but really
isn't. If you're reading this on paper, well, trust me, it's a very
sneaky redirection of a common link.) Unless you've received
a link from a very trusted source – and even then – don't click
it before you check it. I'll explain a simple three-second method to check it further into this handbook.

15.3 ***Unguessable Passwords.*** Really? You're still using your
wife's birthday as your password? While it's a good hab-
it to update your passwords regularly, doing so is less im-

portant than having an un-guessable, complex one. Advice about changing passwords every 90 days is, in my opinion, faulty and gives users a false sense of security. If your password is "pa$$word123" and you change it every 90 days to "pa$$word456," it doesn't make it any less guessable.

15.4 *Password Managers.* Moreover, in today's world, nobody expects you to remember a password anymore. That's what password managers are for. Whether you use the built-in tool in most Windows and Mac computers or a standalone password manager – and there are many to choose from – allow it to generate a complex, long password for you and use a different one for every website and login portal. I have complex passwords that couldn't be cracked by the most powerful computers in 4 billion years. That's a number I can live with. Want to find out how strong your password really is? Enter it here: https://www.security.org/how-secure-is-my-password/.

16 CONFIDENTIALITY, INTEGRITY, & AVAILABILITY

So what does it actually mean to protect your company? It's all about what the experts refer to as the "CIA Triad." No, it doesn't have anything to do with the Central Intelligence Agency (as far as we know, but with those guys...). Rather, it refers to three principal aspects of cybersecurity – Confidentiality, Integrity, & Availability. Whoever is in charge of protecting your company from cyberattacks has to be myopically focused on these three things. Anything else they do is completely useless.

16.1 *Confidentiality* means that whatever you want to keep secret stays secret. Whether it's secret from the outside world or unauthorized people within your own company doesn't matter. If you can't specifically determine who should and should not have access to your information or control over your network, systems, or websites, you have failed.

16.2 *Integrity* means that the data you collect and retain, or the systems you operate and manage, remain intact.

16.3 *Availability* is a simple concept but far more difficult to implement. Having the availability of your data or access to your systems when needed means preventing things like "distributed denial of service" (DDoS) attacks, ransomware, and malicious hacking. If your data isn't available when needed by whoever needs it and however they're supposed to get it, you have failed.

17 ANNUAL CYBERSECURITY REPORT

Companies can avoid 99.9% of potential threats if they just enforce a policy of doing the basic things correctly and in a timely fashion. Simple things such as applying security patches and understanding which devices are authorized to connect to the network will go a long way. A quarterly or at least annual report from the IT department or anyone directly responsible for cybersecurity at the company with evidence of this would be to the benefit of the company.

What to ask
- What training do we give our employees?
- How frequently do we do it?
- What are the results of testing our employees not to do things that endanger our company, such as clicking on unknown links and responding to emails that are not verified to have come from the address that appears?

What to know
- Resistance in cybersecurity is the same as resistance when protecting your home and property.
- Make it as difficult as you can for a hacker to breach your system, and they will move to an easier target.

2022 Crime Types

By Victim Count

Crime Type	Victims	Crime Type	Victims
Phishing	300,497	Government Impersonation	11,554
Personal Data Breach	58,859	Advanced Fee	11,264
Non-Payment/Non-Delivery	51,679	Other	9,966
Extortion	39,416	Overpayment	6,183
Tech Support	32,538	Lottery/Sweepstakes/Inheritance	5,650
Investment	30,529	Data Breach	2,795
Identity Theft	27,922	Crimes Against Children	2,587
Credit Card/Check Fraud	22,985	Ransomware	2,385
BEC	21,832	Threats of Violence	2,224
Spoofing	20,649	I PR/Copyright/Counterfeit	2,183
Confidence/Romance	19,021	SIM Swap	2,026
Employment	14,946	Malware	762
Harassment/Stalking	11,779	Bot net	568
Real Estate	11,727		

RESTRICT

VULNERABILITIES

Limiting access to various functions and services is the best way to restrict what a hacker can do when they successfully breach your system. There are a few vulnerabilities that you can either minimize or eliminate that will help restrict access to your network and data. They include:

1 DATA BROKERS

Data brokers are companies or organizations that collect, aggregate, and sell large volumes of personal information and data from various public and private sources, such as online activities, social media profiles, public records, purchase histories, and more. Data brokers analyze, organize, and package this data into comprehensive profiles that can be sold to other businesses, marketers, advertisers, or even individuals.

The potential dangers posed by data brokers to both companies' and individuals' cybersecurity include:

1.1 *Privacy Risks*. Data brokers amass vast amounts of personal information, which can include names, addresses, contact details, demographic information, browsing habits, and even sensitive information like financial records or medical history. This concentration of personal data increases the risk of privacy breaches if the data falls into the wrong hands or is misused.

1.2 *Targeted Cyberattacks*. Cybercriminals and malicious actors can target data brokers to gain access to the extensive data repositories they maintain. Breaching a data broker's systems allows attackers to access a wealth of personal information that can be exploited for various malicious activities, such as identity theft, phishing, social engineering, or fraud.

1.3 *Data Breaches & Exposure*. Data brokers, like any other entities that collect and store large volumes of personal information, are also susceptible to data breaches. If a data broker's systems are compromised, it can result in the exposure of vast amounts of personal data, leading to potential harm to individuals' privacy, financial security, or even reputation.

1.4 *Profiling & Surveillance.* Data brokers create detailed profiles based on collected data, which can be used for targeted advertising, marketing campaigns, or even surveillance purposes. This level of profiling raises concerns about the erosion of personal privacy, as individuals may not be aware of the extent of data collected or how it is used to track their activities and preferences.

1.5 *Social Engineering Attacks.* The information collected and aggregated by data brokers can be used to craft sophisticated social engineering attacks. Cybercriminals can leverage personal details to create personalized phishing emails, messages, or phone calls that appear legitimate, increasing the likelihood of successful attacks or tricking individuals into revealing sensitive information.

For companies, the risks associated with data brokers lie in the potential exposure of sensitive business data, intellectual property, or customer information. Companies may unwittingly share valuable information with data brokers, and if this data falls into the wrong hands, it can lead to competitive disadvantages, financial losses, or reputational damage.

To mitigate the risks associated with data brokers, both individuals and companies can consider the following actions:

➤ *Limit Data Sharing.* Be cautious when providing personal information online and consider the necessity of sharing sensitive details. Opt out of data broker services whenever possible.

➤ *Data Privacy Practices.* Implement robust privacy practices, including strong passwords, two-factor authentication, and regular monitoring of personal accounts for suspicious activities.

➤ *Regular Monitoring.* Regularly review your online presence, privacy settings, and permissions granted to third-party applications or services. Be aware of the information shared and accessible through these channels.

▸ *Regulatory Compliance*. Stay informed about privacy laws and regulations in your jurisdiction, such as the General Data Protection Regulation (GDPR) in the European Union or the California Consumer Privacy Act (CCPA) in the United States. Understand your rights and how data brokers handle personal information under these regulations.

By being vigilant and proactive in managing personal data and understanding the risks associated with data brokers, individuals and companies can better protect themselves from potential cybersecurity threats and privacy breaches.

2 STATE-SPONSORED "ACTORS"

A state-sponsored actor refers to an individual or group that is supported, funded, or directed by a nation-state to conduct cyber attacks or engage in other malicious activities. These actors are backed by substantial resources, including technical expertise, advanced technologies, and financial backing from their sponsoring government. State-sponsored attacks are typically motivated by political, economic, or military objectives and can pose significant challenges for targeted entities. Here's why their attacks may be particularly difficult to resist or repel.

2.1 *Advanced Capabilities*. State-sponsored actors often possess advanced capabilities and access to cutting-edge technologies, zero-day vulnerabilities, and specialized techniques that are not readily available to common cybercriminals. This makes their attacks more sophisticated, difficult to detect, and challenging to defend against.

2.2 *Intelligence & Reconnaissance*. State-sponsored actors invest significant time and effort in conducting thorough intelligence gathering and reconnaissance activities before launching an attack. They carefully study their targets, identifying vulnerabilities, weaknesses, and potential entry points. This comprehensive understanding of the target increases the effectiveness of their attacks and makes them harder to anticipate or prevent.

2.3 *Persistence & Resources.* State-sponsored actors are typically persistent in their attacks. They can dedicate substantial resources and time to compromise their targets, often employing multiple attack vectors simultaneously. They may engage in long-term campaigns, patiently conducting reconnaissance, establishing footholds, and gradually escalating their access until they achieve their objectives. This persistence can make it difficult for organizations to detect and mitigate the attacks.

2.4 *Nation-State Backing.* State-sponsored actors operate with the support and resources of a nation-state, which grants them certain advantages. They may benefit from legal protections, intelligence agencies, and diplomatic cover that can complicate efforts to hold them accountable or disrupt their operations. Additionally, they may have access to government infrastructure, critical information, or insider knowledge that can facilitate their attacks and evade detection.

2.5 *Global Reach.* State-sponsored actors often operate across international borders, leveraging global networks and infrastructure to conduct their activities. They can launch attacks from multiple jurisdictions, making it challenging for law enforcement and security agencies to coordinate and respond effectively. This cross-border nature can create legal and jurisdictional complexities, further hindering efforts to resist or repel their attacks.

2.6 *Collateral Damage & Escalation.* State-sponsored attacks can have wider implications beyond the immediate targets. They can inadvertently cause collateral damage to other organizations, critical infrastructure, or even citizens. Moreover, if attacks escalate between nations, there is a risk of a broader cyber conflict, potentially resulting in economic disruptions, disruption of essential services, or even physical damage.

Effectively defending against state-sponsored attacks requires a multi-layered and holistic approach. This includes robust cybersecurity measures such as regular patching, network segmentation, strong access controls, intrusion detection systems, and incident response plans. Additionally, international cooperation and information sharing among governments, intelligence agencies, and private sector entities are crucial to detect, attribute, and respond to state-sponsored attacks.

RESTRICTIONS

There are some simple, effective things you can do to restrict what hackers can do when they attempt to breach your system or even after they're already in. They include:

1 TWO-FACTOR AUTHENTICATION

Two-factor authentication (2FA) is a security measure that adds an extra layer of protection to your online accounts beyond just a username and password. It helps ensure that only you can access your accounts, even if someone else manages to obtain your login credentials.

Here's how it works: When you enable 2FA for an account, such as your email or social media, you need to provide two different pieces of information to verify your identity. The first factor is typically something you know, like your password. The second factor is something you have, like a physical device or an app on your smartphone.

One commonly used method of 2FA is SMS-based authentication. When you log in to your account, after entering your password, you receive a text message with a unique code on your registered phone number. You then enter this code into the login screen to complete the authentication process. This ensures that even if someone guesses or steals your password, they would still need access to your phone to receive the code.

2 AUTHENTICATION APPS

Another method is using authentication apps, such as Duo, Google Authenticator or Authy. After setting up 2FA, when you log in to your account, the app generates a time-based one-time code that you need to enter along with your password. The code changes every few seconds, adding an extra layer of security. This means that even if someone has your password, they can't log in without the current code from the app.

Both SMS 2FA and authentication apps provide an additional barrier against unauthorized access to your accounts. By requiring multiple factors for authentication, 2FA significantly enhances the security of your online presence.

3 USING A VPN

Think of a VPN as a private tunnel that you use to access the internet. When you connect to a VPN, your data travels through this tunnel, protected by walls and locks, shielding it from prying eyes. It's as if you're in a secret passageway that encrypts your online activities and disguises your location. This secure tunnel ensures that your internet connection remains private and secure, allowing you to browse the web, access restricted content, and communicate with others without worrying about your data falling into the wrong hands.

❖ DEEP DIVE

A VPN (Virtual Private Network) is a technology that creates a secure and encrypted connection over a public network, such as the internet. It allows users to send and receive data as if they were directly connected to a private network, even while using a public or untrusted network.

Here's a breakdown of how a VPN works:

3.1 *Secure Connection*. When you connect to a VPN, your device establishes a secure and encrypted connection to a VPN server located in a different location. This connection is protected with advanced encryption protocols, ensuring that your data remains confidential and secure.

3.2 *Privacy & Anonymity*. Once connected to a VPN, your internet traffic is routed through the VPN server before reaching its destination. This means that your IP address, which reveals your location and identity, is masked and replaced with the IP address of the VPN server, enhancing privacy and anonymity and making it more difficult for others to track or identify your online activities.

3.3 *Encryption*. A key feature of VPNs is encryption. All data transmitted between your device and the VPN server is encrypted, making it unreadable to anyone who may intercept it. Encryption ensures that even if your data is intercepted, it is effectively scrambled and protected from unauthorized access.

3.4 *Bypassing Restrictions*. VPNs allow you to bypass geographical restrictions or censorship imposed by governments, internet service providers (ISPs), or other entities. By connecting to a VPN server in a different country, you can access websites, services, or content that may be restricted or unavailable in your current location.

3.5 *Secure Remote Access*. VPNs enable secure remote access to private networks. For example, employees working from home or remote locations can use a VPN to connect securely to their organization's internal network and access resources as if they were physically present in the office. This ensures data confidentiality and allows for secure communication and collaboration.

It's important to note that while VPNs provide a secure and private connection, they don't guarantee absolute anonymity or protection from all types of threats. VPN security depends on various factors, including the encryption protocols used, the VPN provider's trustworthiness, and the user's own security practices.

4 ADVANTAGES OF A VPN

In summary, a VPN creates a secure and encrypted tunnel between your device and a VPN server, allowing you to browse the internet privately, bypass restrictions, and securely access remote networks. It offers an extra layer of security and privacy, making it a valuable tool for protecting your online activities and sensitive data. From a corporate cybersecurity standpoint, there are several benefits of having a Virtual Private Network (VPN) and imposing its use, especially for people who work remotely. Here are some key advantages.

4.1 *Secure Remote Access.* A VPN establishes an encrypted and secure connection between remote employees and the corporate network. It ensures that sensitive data transmitted over public networks, such as the internet, remains protected from eavesdropping and interception. By using a VPN, remote workers can securely access company resources, databases, and internal systems, reducing the risk of data breaches or unauthorized access.

4.2 *Data Protection.* VPNs provide an additional layer of data protection by encrypting all traffic transmitted between remote devices and the corporate network. This encryption makes it difficult for attackers to intercept and decipher sensitive information, such as login credentials, financial data, or confidential documents. It helps mitigate the risks associated with unsecured public Wi-Fi networks often used by remote workers.

4.3 *Secure Communication Channels.* VPNs create a secure and private communication channel between remote workers and the corporate network. This ensures that communications, including emails, file transfers, and video conferences, are protected from unauthorized access or surveillance. This security particularly important for organizations dealing with sensitive or regulated data, as it helps maintain compliance with data protection regulations.

4.4 *Protection Against Network-Based Attacks.* VPNs offer protection against network-based attacks, such as man-in-the-middle attacks or DNS spoofing. By encrypting traffic and routing it through secure tunnels, VPNs make it difficult for attackers to tamper with or intercept data packets. This adds an extra layer of defense, safeguarding remote workers from common network-based threats.

(DNS spoofing is a technique used by malicious actors to trick your computer or device into going to the wrong website. Imagine you want to visit a specific website by typing its name into your web browser. Normally, your computer asks a DNS server for the correct address of that website, just like asking for directions to a place. DNS spoofing happens when someone manipulates the DNS system and gives your computer the wrong address, leading you to a fake website that looks similar to the real one. This can be dangerous because the fake website might try to steal your personal information, like passwords or credit card details. It's like someone putting up fake road signs, directing you to the wrong destination, where they can deceive or harm you.)

4.5 *Enhanced Identity & Access Management.* VPNs, when integrated with proper identity and access management (IAM) practices, enable organizations to enforce stronger authentication measures. By requiring employees to authenticate themselves using multi-factor authentication (MFA) or digital certificates to establish a VPN connection, organizations can significantly reduce the risk of unauthorized access and improve overall access control.

4.6 *Regulatory Compliance.* In regulated industries, such as healthcare, finance, or legal sectors, VPNs can assist in meeting specific compliance requirements. They help protect sensitive customer information and maintain the confidentiality and integrity of data during transmission. Adhering to regulatory standards not only avoids potential fines or penalties but also demonstrates a commitment to data privacy and security.

By imposing the use of VPNs for remote workers, organizations can enforce a consistent and secure approach to remote access. It ensures that all communication and data transmission from remote locations adhere to the same robust security standards as on-site operations. This helps mitigate the risks associated with remote work and strengthens the overall cybersecurity posture of the organization.

5 ZERO TRUST

Zero trust is a cybersecurity approach that challenges the traditional belief of "trust but verify." In a zero-trust model, the fundamental principle is to assume that no user or device within a network is inherently trustworthy, regardless of their location or previous credentials. Instead, zero trust promotes a comprehensive verification process for every user, device, and network interaction.

Imagine it as a security philosophy that constantly questions and verifies the identity and intentions of anyone or anything seeking access to sensitive information or resources. It's like having multiple layers of digital checkpoints that rigorously assess and authorize each request before granting access. This approach helps protect against potential threats and reduces the risks of unauthorized access, even if an attacker manages to breach one layer of defense.

In a zero-trust architecture, key elements such as user identity, device health, network context, and behavioral patterns are thoroughly examined before granting access to specific resources. This ensures that only authenticated and authorized individuals or devices can access sensitive data or systems, regardless of their location or whether they are inside or outside the traditional network perimeter.

By adopting a zero-trust mindset, organizations enhance their security posture by minimizing the potential impact of a breach and reducing the likelihood of lateral movement within their networks. It helps create a more resilient cybersecurity framework that focuses on continuous authentication and strict access controls to safeguard critical assets in an increasingly interconnected and dynamic digital landscape.

6 PRINCIPLE OF LEAST PRIVILEGE

The principle of least privilege is another important concept in cybersecurity. It revolves around the idea of granting users, applications, or systems the minimum level of access necessary to perform their required tasks and nothing more.

Imagine you have a building with different rooms, each containing valuable resources or sensitive information. The principle of least privilege suggests that individuals should only have access to the specific rooms they need to do their job and no more. For example, if someone's role only requires access to the accounting department, they shouldn't be granted access to other areas such as human resources or executive offices.

Applying this principle to cybersecurity means that user accounts, applications, or systems are given only the privileges or permissions essential for their designated functions. By limiting access rights to the bare minimum, the potential damage caused by accidental or intentional misuse or abuse is greatly reduced. This approach minimizes the attack surface and mitigates the risk of unauthorized access or malicious activities.

The principle of least privilege promotes a proactive and security-focused mindset, ensuring that access controls are designed and implemented with careful consideration. It encourages organizations to regularly review and update access permissions on a "need to know" basis and closely monitor user activities to detect any suspicious behavior.

Overall, the principle of least privilege helps enhance the security and integrity of systems and data by limiting access rights to only what is necessary, reducing the potential for human error, insider threats, or unauthorized access attempts. Avoid the single point of failure problem:

Does the organization have a single point of failure? It could be something as simple as a power supply or as complex as a succession plan for the IT department's key personnel. What if a specific vendor goes bankrupt? If the hosting company you're using for your website is at risk, so are you. If they are exposed to their own single point of failure or get disconnected due to financial problems, what happens to your website? Are you backed up to the point where you have a copy of your own site so that you can host it yourself in an emergency? A business analysis will be required to determine whether the potential risk – and cost to remediate – a single point of failure is worthwhile when compared to the damage it might cause.

What to ask
- What method(s) do we use to isolate areas of access?
- Do we have policies that handle access revocation when someone exits the company?

What to know
There are multiple methods of restricting access to various parts of your system if the initial perimeter protection is breached. Like water-lock compartments on a ship that prevent it from sinking if there is a leak in the hull, it's essential to compartmentalize individual areas of your system.

RECOVER

IN TODAY'S WORLD of cybersecurity, the concept of recovery and backup refers to more than just the importance of having plans and systems in place to restore data and operations after a security incident or other disruptive event. It also refers to another "R" - Resilience. The ability to bounce back from attacks, or to "self-heal" after an attack is discovered, is an important aspect of your cybersecurity planning.

Imagine you have important files, documents, or even cherished memories stored on your computer or mobile device. Now, consider what would happen if your device suddenly stopped working, got stolen, or became infected with malware. Without a backup, you would potentially lose all that valuable information, and it might be challenging or even impossible to recover it.

Recovery and backups are like a safety net for your digital world. They involve creating duplicate copies of your important data and storing them in a secure and separate location. These backups act as a reliable source to restore your information in case of a cyber attack, hardware failure, accidental deletion, or any other unexpected event that may cause data loss.

1 BACKUPS

Having a backup strategy is vital for four reasons:

1.1 *Data Protection*. Backups provide a layer of protection against data loss. If your primary data is compromised, you can retrieve and restore it from the backup copies, ensuring that you don't permanently lose critical information.

1.2 *Business Continuity*. For organizations, backups are crucial for maintaining uninterrupted operations. If a cyber incident disrupts your systems or makes data inaccessible, having backups allows you to recover quickly, minimize downtime, and continue serving your customers without major disruptions.

1.3 *Ransomware Defense*. Backups can also be a valuable defense against ransomware attacks. If your data is encrypted and held hostage by cybercriminals, having up-to-date backups allows you to restore your systems and data without paying the ransom.

1.4 *Peace of Mind*. Knowing that you have backups gives you peace of mind. You can rest assured that even if something unfortunate happens to your devices or data, you have a plan in place to recover and restore everything as it was.

To implement a backup strategy, you can use methods such as external hard drives, cloud storage services, or specialized backup software. It's essential to regularly update and test your backups to ensure they are reliable and up-to-date.

2 DOCUMENTS

In addition to backups, there are three documents that every company should have available in the event of a breach.

2.1 *Network Diagrams*. This is like a map that shows how all the different devices and computers in a network are connected to each other. It helps everyone understand the layout of the network, which is important for managing and securing it effectively. This diagram can include things like routers, switches, servers, and computers, and it helps identify potential weak points or vulnerabilities that need protection.

2.2 *Data Flow Diagrams*. A data flow diagram (DFD) is a visual representation that shows how data moves within a system or organization. In cybersecurity terms, a DFD helps you understand how data is collected, processed, stored, and transmitted across different parts of a network or system. In a DFD, data is typically represented as arrows, and various components or processes in the system are represented as circles or rectangles. The arrows indicate the flow of data between these components. This diagram helps in analyzing and documenting how data is accessed and used, which is crucial for cybersecurity professionals to identify potential security risks and protect sensitive information.

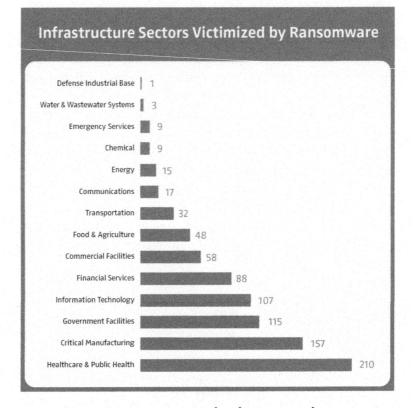

Infrastructure Sectors Victimized by Ransomware

Sector	Count
Defense Industrial Base	1
Water & Wastewater Systems	3
Emergency Services	9
Chemical	9
Energy	15
Communications	17
Transportation	32
Food & Agriculture	48
Commercial Facilities	58
Financial Services	88
Information Technology	107
Government Facilities	115
Critical Manufacturing	157
Healthcare & Public Health	210

2.3 *Data Map Documents.* Also known as data mapping documents or data mapping diagrams, are documents or visual representations that provide a detailed view of how data flows within an organization, particularly as it moves between different systems, applications, or databases. These documents typically include information about:

➤ *Data Sources* (where the data originates, such as databases, applications, or external sources like customer forms)

➤ *Data Destinations* (where the data is sent or stored, such as other databases, analytics platforms, or reporting tools)

➤ *Data Transformation* (any changes or conversions that happen to the data during its journey, like format changes or calculations),

➤ *Data Relationships* (how different pieces of data are related to each other) and Data Security (information about data access controls, encryption, and other security measures in place to protect the data).

(Note to the legal folks. It's essential for the legal department in every enterprise to know in advance what laws apply to various types of data breaches that might happen to them. In the unfortunate event of a data breach, there will be so much else to handle that you will want to have this at your fingertips. Keep this ready and updated to avoid last-minute confusion or errors if the situation arises. Note that most laws that regulate what has to be revealed if a breach occurs make exceptions if the data is encrypted. This is another good reason to keep all of the data in the organization encrypted when at rest or in transit. If the system is breached but the data is encrypted, you may be exempt from having to report or reveal the incident.)

In summary, recovery and backups are essential because they protect your valuable data, enable business continuity, defend against ransomware, and provide peace of mind. They are like a safety net that ensures you have a way to restore your digital life even in the face of unexpected cyber incidents or data loss.

RESILIENCE

NOW LET'S TALK about an associated "R" – Resilience. Resilience is a crucial concept in cybersecurity that plays a vital role in protecting our digital systems and information. Resilience refers to the ease and speed of recovery or how the system self-heals after a breach.

In the digital world we live in, we rely on various technologies, such as computers, smartphones, and online services, to store and access our personal and sensitive information. However, these systems are constantly under the threat of cyberattacks, which can lead to unauthorized access, data breaches, or service disruptions.

Resilience refers to the ability of our digital systems to withstand and recover from these cyberattacks or any other unexpected events. It involves implementing measures and strategies to minimize the impact of an attack and to ensure the continuity of our systems and data.

1 IMPORTANCE OF RESILIENCE
Here are a few reasons why resilience is important:

1.1 *Protection of Personal Information*. Resilience measures help safeguard your personal and sensitive information from falling into the wrong hands. By implementing security controls and backup systems, resilience helps ensure that even if an attack occurs, your data remains protected.

1.2 *Continuity of Services*. In our interconnected world, many aspects of our lives rely on digital services like online banking, e-commerce, or communication platforms. Resilience helps maintain the availability and functionality of these services, even in the face of cyberattacks or other disruptions, ensuring that you can continue to access the services you need for your studies, work, or personal activities.

1.3 *Mitigating Financial Losses*. Cyberattacks can have significant financial implications for individuals and organizations. By investing in resilience measures, we can reduce the

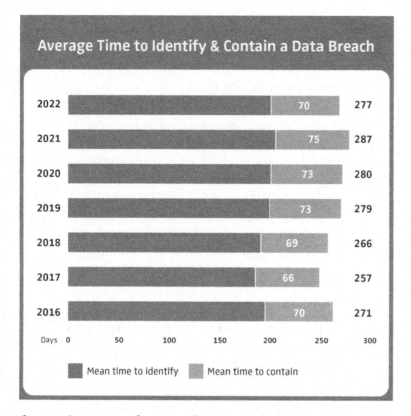

Average Time to Identify & Contain a Data Breach

Year	Mean time to contain	Total
2022	70	277
2021	75	287
2020	73	280
2019	73	279
2018	69	266
2017	66	257
2016	70	271

Days 0   50   100   150   200   250   300

■ Mean time to identify   ■ Mean time to contain

financial impact of an attack. This includes proactive steps such as regular backups, employing secure technologies, and having incident response plans in place to minimize downtime and recovery costs.

1.4 *Safeguarding Trust*. Resilience in cybersecurity helps build and maintain trust in our digital systems. When individuals and organizations have confidence in the security and resilience of the technologies they use, they are more likely to engage in online activities, share information, and participate in the digital economy.

By understanding the importance of resilience in cybersecurity, you can make informed decisions about protecting your personal information, adopting secure practices, and supporting organizations that prioritize resilience. It is essential to stay vigilant, follow best practices, and regularly update your devices and software to help maintain a resilient digital environment.

2 BUSINESS CONTINUITY PLAN

A Business Continuity Plan is crucial for recovery. The next important cybersecurity consideration is your Business Continuity Plan (BCP). You might know how the business will continue to run or get back up if there is a disaster, but do you know how to handle a cyber-disaster? Is the organization fully prepared for all facilities to go offline due to natural events such as earthquakes, lightning strikes, fires, or floods? If so, is it also prepared to work after a cyberattack has disabled systems, encrypted files, stopped email and prevented payroll from processing? Having a cybersecurity business continuity plan is like doing really thorough fire drills – when it occurs (and it almost certainly will occur) you'll know how to handle it because you will have already handled it by practicing.

The benefits of having a cyber business continuity plan are numerous:

2.1 *Minimizing Downtime*. A BCP helps minimize the impact of unforeseen events, such as natural disasters, cyberattacks, or system failures. By having a plan in place, businesses can swiftly respond to disruptions and reduce downtime, ultimately minimizing financial losses and preserving customer trust.

2.2 *Maintaining Service & Operations*. A well-designed BCP ensures that essential services and operations can continue even during adverse events. By identifying key processes, dependencies, and necessary resources in advance, organizations can develop strategies to sustain their operations, provide uninterrupted services, and meet customer demands, thereby minimizing disruption to their customers and stakeholders.

2.3 *Enhancing Resilience*. A BCP promotes organizational resilience by improving the ability to adapt and recover quickly from disruptive incidents. It enables businesses to proactively identify vulnerabilities, assess potential risks, and implement measures to mitigate them. By being prepared, organizations can effectively navigate challenging circumstances, protecting their reputation and competitive advantage.

2.4 *Safeguarding Data & Assets.* A key aspect of a BCP is ensuring the protection and integrity of critical data, systems, and assets. By implementing robust backup and recovery procedures, data encryption, off-site storage, and other security measures, organizations can safeguard their valuable information and resources from threats such as data breaches, theft, or physical damage.

2.5 *Meeting Regulatory & Compliance Requirements.* Many industries have regulatory and compliance obligations that require organizations to have a BCP in place. By developing and implementing a comprehensive plan, businesses can demonstrate their commitment to meeting these requirements, reducing the risk of penalties, legal issues, or reputational damage.

2.6 *Enhancing Employee Safety & Well-Being.* A BCP also considers the safety and well-being of employees during emergencies. It provides guidelines and procedures for evacuation, emergency communication, and ensuring their welfare. By prioritizing employee safety, organizations demonstrate their commitment to their workforce, fostering a positive work environment.

Overall, a business continuity plan provides a framework for effective crisis management, risk mitigation, and operational resilience. It helps businesses navigate unexpected events, protect their assets, and maintain customer satisfaction. By investing time and resources in creating a robust BCP, organizations can ensure they are well-prepared to withstand and recover from various disruptions, ultimately enhancing their long-term success.

3 CRISIS MANAGEMENT TEAM
There is one last thing to add to the Business Continuity Plan

that you won't find mentioned in most technical explanations – you need a crisis management team on "speed dial" (an interesting technological anachronism because nobody "dials" numbers anymore and "speed dial" is an old concept that is largely irrelevant to the smartphone-using public). Why? To help handle the impacts of any attack and remove the burden of public-facing conversations (see "REPORT" below) that deal with employees, shareholders, media, etc.

From the perspective of a Director or CEO, having a crisis management team available when a breach occurs offers several benefits.

3.1 *Rapid Response & Minimized Impact*. A crisis management team brings expertise and experience in handling cybersecurity incidents. Their immediate involvement enables a swift response to the breach, which minimizes the potential impact on the organization's operations, reputation, and customer trust.

3.2 *Effective Incident Containment & Mitigation*. A specialized crisis management team understands the intricacies of cyber incidents and can effectively contain and mitigate the breach. They can assess the scope and severity of the breach, identify vulnerabilities, and implement remediation measures promptly to prevent further damage.

3.3 *Coordinated Communication & Public Relations*. Breaches often require transparent and timely communication with stakeholders, including customers, employees, partners, regulatory bodies, and the media. A crisis management team can help develop and execute an effective communication strategy, managing public relations and ensuring consistent messaging throughout the incident response process.

3.4 *Compliance & Legal Guidance*. Cybersecurity breaches may have legal implications and require compliance with various regulations and disclosure requirements. A crisis management team can provide legal guidance, ensuring that the organization meets its legal obligations and navigates any potential regulatory consequences effectively.

3.5 *Lessons Learned & Post-Incident Analysis.* A crisis management team plays a vital role in conducting post-incident analysis and capturing lessons learned. They can assess the root causes of the breach, identify vulnerabilities in existing security measures, and provide recommendations to enhance the organization's cybersecurity posture for the future.

4 ENGAGING A CRISIS MANAGEMENT TEAM

Engaging a crisis management team in advance is highly recommended. Preparing for a breach by establishing a relationship with a trusted firm helps ensure a timely and efficient response when an incident occurs. Waiting until an incident happens can lead to delays in response, unpreparedness, and an increased risk of prolonged disruption.

When selecting a crisis management firm, consider the following factors.

4.1 *Expertise & Experience.* Look for a firm with extensive experience in cybersecurity incident response and crisis management. They should have a track record of handling breaches across various industries.

4.2 *Proactive Approach.* Seek a firm that emphasizes proactive incident response planning, including the development of comprehensive response playbooks, tabletop exercises, and ongoing training for your organization.

4.3 *Availability & Response Time.* Ensure the firm can provide timely assistance during an incident. Prompt response and availability are crucial in minimizing the impact of a breach.

4.4 *Communication & Reporting.* Evaluate the firm's capabilities in managing internal and external communication during a crisis. They should be able to assist with crafting messages, handling media inquiries, and providing regular updates to stakeholders.

Once you have identified a suitable crisis management firm, establish a clear working arrangement by.

▸ *Defining Roles and Responsibilities.* Clearly outline the roles and responsibilities of both your internal team and the crisis management firm during an incident. Establish communication channels and escalation paths to facilitate effective collaboration.

➤ *Developing an Incident Response Plan.* Work with the crisis management firm to develop an incident response plan tailored to your organization's specific needs. The plan should outline step-by-step procedures, contact information, and predefined decision-making processes.

➤ *Conducting Exercises and Training.* Regularly conduct tabletop exercises and training sessions to ensure your internal team is familiar with the incident response plan and can collaborate effectively with the crisis management firm.

By engaging a crisis management team in advance and establishing a solid working relationship, your organization can effectively respond to cybersecurity incidents, minimize their impact, and swiftly restore normal operations.

REPORT

1 WHY REPORT?

It might be painful to do, but it's essential to report any breach or intrusion as soon as possible to the board and later to the public or shareholders for several reasons:

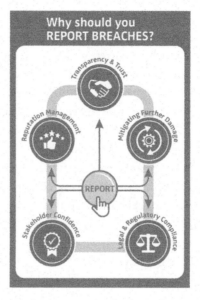

1.1 *Transparency & Trust.* By promptly disclosing a breach or intrusion, the company demonstrates transparency & honesty, which helps build trust with customers, stakeholders, and shareholders. It shows that the organization takes cybersecurity seriously and is committed to protecting sensitive information.

1.2 *Mitigating Further Damage.* Reporting a breach allows affected individuals to take necessary actions to protect themselves, such as changing passwords or monitoring their accounts for suspicious activity. It also enables the company to implement additional security measures to prevent further damage and similar future incidents.

1.3 *Legal & Regulatory Compliance.* Many jurisdictions have laws and regulations that require organizations to disclose data breaches or security incidents. Compliance with these laws is crucial to avoid legal consequences and financial penalties. Reporting the breach also demonstrates the company's commitment to meeting its legal obligations.

1.4 *Reputation Management.* Failing to report a breach can have severe reputational repercussions. If the breach becomes public through other means, such as media coverage or word-of-mouth, it can lead to a loss of trust, negative publicity, and potential damage to the company's brand. By pro-actively disclosing the breach, the company can control the narrative and actively manage its reputation.

1.5 *Stakeholder Confidence.* Shareholders and investors need to be informed about any cybersecurity incidents that may impact the company's operations or financial standing. Prompt reporting allows them to assess the potential risks and take appropriate actions. Open communication fosters confidence in the company's management and decision-making processes.

Overall, reporting breaches or intrusions promptly and transparently is essential for maintaining trust, mitigating damage, complying with legal requirements, managing reputation, and instilling confidence in customers, stakeholders, and shareholders. It is a responsible and necessary step in today's cybersecurity landscape.

2 HOW TO REPORT

So, just how should you report a breach, the loss of data or compromised privacy of data? There are several steps but the first thing to remember is that this should be handled carefully and in compliance with relevant laws and regulations, as well as considering the best interests of affected individuals and your organization's reputation. Here are some suggested steps to report a data breach:

2.1 *Internal Assessment.* First, conduct a thorough internal assessment to determine the scope and nature of the breach. Identify what data was compromised, how it happened, and assess the potential impact.

2.2 *Determine Legal & Regulatory Compliance.* Consult with legal counsel to ensure compliance with data breach notification laws in your jurisdiction. Some laws require prompt notification to affected individuals, regulatory authorities, or both.

2.3 *Notify Affected Individuals*. If required by law or best practices – or your personal commitment to your customers, vendors, employees – notify affected individuals promptly and provide information on the breach, its potential consequences, and steps they can take to protect themselves.

2.4 *Notify Relevant Authorities*. Report the breach to relevant regulatory authorities or data protection agencies as required by law.

2.5 *Communicate*. While a news release isn't always necessary, it may be appropriate if the breach is significant or likely to attract media attention. Consider the impact on your organization's reputation and the public's right to know.

2.6 *Website Notices*. Posting notices on your website can be a way to provide information to affected individuals and the public. This can include details about the breach, steps taken to address it, and resources for affected individuals.

2.7 *Customer Support*. Offer a dedicated support channel for affected individuals to address their concerns and questions.

Remember that the specific actions you take may vary depending on the nature and severity of the breach, applicable laws, and the policies of your organization. It's essential to prioritize the protection and support of affected individuals and to be transparent about the breach's impact while being mindful of your organization's reputation.

Reports shouldn't be limited to just after a breach occurs when you need damage control. Reports, especially to the board, should be done quarterly using specific metrics such as compliance accomplishments, for example, "We are now ISO-27001 compliant" (What does that mean? https://www.iso.org/isoiec-27001-information-security.html).

Other metrics and details quarterly reports should contain include:

➤ *General.* What is our risk tolerance?

➤ *General.* Are we providing the right training to the right people?

➤ *General.* How long does it take to remove employee network and facilities access?

➤ *General.* On a scale of 1–10, how strong are our passwords?

➤ *General.* When was our last cyber review or penetration test?

➤ *General.* Do we have the right negotiating skills in case ransomware can't be avoided?

➤ *Statistical.* What percentage of users click on spearphishing training emails?

➤ *Technical.* What is our latency on patch installation? How many "versions" behind are we?

➤ *Technical.* What is our mean time to detect and respond to breaches?

What to ask

Be sure to have the individual in charge of the company's cybersecurity (CTO, CISO, VP Technology) meet with the board quarterly to provide an update and ask the questions listed above

What to know

- Reporting can be painful, but it's essential to do it quickly.
- Reporting should be more than just part of damage control. Reports, especially to a board, should be done regularly.

A FINAL NOTE

IN THE END, cybersecurity isn't really about software or hardware. It isn't about bad links, viruses or backups. It's not even about hackers and IT departments and regulations. It's about having the right attitude, the mental state, the culture of protecting yourself and your company. We've had it pretty easy for a long time in just the same way that homeowners could, long ago, leave doors unlocked when they left for the day. Now you need to lock both your real doors and the metaphorical ones. And you have to make sure there are no loose keys floating around and that your valuables are well hidden in case someone does get into your house.

Your company, your data, your privacy – that's your house now. You can protect it pretty effectively just being aware. In this case, by being "cyberaware."

If you remember nothing else from this book just remember the Four Rs: *Resist, Restrict, Recover and Report*. By remembering just those key words you'll always know what to ask, what to know and what to ignore. As a non-geek in today's world, they will guide you.

In short, to stay one step ahead of the bad guys be careful, be diligent and be cyberaware!

RECAPITULATION

The text face used in this book is Garalda, a humanist
slab serif font family designed by Xavier Dupré
and issued by TypeTogether
in 2016.

❖

Contact Scott Goldman directly at
BeCyberAware@iCloud.com